THE EXPERT'S GUIDE™

To Surviving Your Marriage

by
SAM PRIEST
Illustrated by James Angus

S.p.i. BOOKS

New York

For further information, contact:

S.P.I. Books
99 Spring Street, 3rd Floor
New York, NY 10012
Tel: (212) 431-5011
Fax: (212) 431-8646
E-mail: publicity@spibooks.com

10 9 8 7 6 5 4 3 2 1
First Edition

Library of Congress Cataloging-in-Publication Date available.

S.P.I. Books World Wide Web address: *www.spibooks.com*

ISBN: 1-56171-925-0

TABLE OF CONTENTS

The first nine years are the worst.

INTRODUCTION

Men who have recently married soon wake up and discover themselves trapped as inmates in a world they did not create and cannot control. Their every move is monitored. They can no longer come and go as they please. And worst of all, they are legally forbidden from doing what they are genetically hard-wired to do—namely, shagging loads of attractive women.

As an inmate in the marital prison, you need help. And we, the folks at *The Expert's Guide™ series*, are here to give it to you. Our lobbyists are working full time in all 50 states to have the institution of marriage abolished. Let's give America what American men really want—a free market for sex. A place where a woman has to hold on to her man on the merits, not because the law has tied him in knots.

But guys, to be honest, it may take a while before our lobbyists succeed in abolishing marriage. To help you survive until then, we have created *The Expert's Guide™ to Surviving Your Marriage*—a breakthrough survival guide for the married man.

There is no sex after marriage.

CHAPTER · I

THE MYTH OF POST-MARITAL SEX

In the old days, people used to ask if you believed in premarital sex.

I do. I have seen it happen.

Post-marital sex is another matter.

Science has now proven that sex between married couples who have been married more than six months is so infrequent as to be statistically insignificant.

But despite all our warnings, you went out and got married. By now, you have probably discovered the First Law of Marital Dynamics:

There Is No Sex After Marriage.

All animals under stress quickly lose interest in sex. The same stresses can quickly destroy a marriage unless an appropriate outlet is found.

Many men say they didn't know what happiness was until they were married. Of course, by then it was too late.

But all is not lost. Marriage does not have to be a life sentence. Many men get out on good behavior in just one or two years. And by following the simple rules set out in this book you can still save your marriage by learning how to cheat on your wife without getting caught.

This book can help you change your patterns and upgrade your mistresses and girlfriends. It can help you to stop having sex with your wife and get the kind of women you really want.

The attractive ones.

Here's how to do it.

"Honey, did you have a chance to pick up my dry cleaning?"

CHAPTER II

WOMEN ARE ATTENTION-GETTING MACHINES

(BUT THEY ARE KIND OF AIMLESS AND BORED)

Before we get started, let's talk about what women want.

• *Women Have Different Goals.*

Men and women want very different things. In order to understand women, you have to know what their goals are. The table set forth below is an easy to remember reference for what she wants. If necessary, tear out this page and put it in your wallet.

Differences Between Men And Women

WHAT YOU WANT	*WHAT SHE WANTS*
1. Sex	1. Attention/love
2. Threesomes	2. Security/commitment
3. Sex	3. An engagement ring
4. Threesomes	4. Children
5. Sex	5. Control over you and your financial resources

The first rule of successful shagging is that if you want a woman you must pay attention to her. Love, sex, money, gifts, compliments, flowers, conversation, dinners and marriage proposals are just forms of attention. The more attention you pay, the better results you will achieve. And *pay* is the operative word.

A woman wants to feel loved. She measures how much you love her by how much attention you give her. If you are not paying enough attention to her, she will think you don't love her.

How much attention is enough?

That's easy. It's *never* enough.

A woman will tend to fall for a man who really likes her (or pretends he does). Often, she will be much more concerned about whether you like her than whether she likes you.

That's also why so many beautiful women end up with ugly old guys. How do these guys get attractive women? By paying attention to them in the form of cash.

• <u>Why Do Women Spend So Much Energy On Their Appearance?</u>

Women are concerned about their appearance because their appearance is how they attract what they want most.

You guessed it: attention!

• _Women Can Be Kind Of Aimless And Bored._

Once she gets your attention, it's up to you to make something happen. She isn't likely to come over and pick you up. _You_ need to do the work.

While attractive women are good at attracting your attention, you will find that they are often kind of aimless and bored. They want you to take charge of entertaining them.

Women are good at waiting. They have to wait to catch your eye and then wait for you to do something about it. And they have no problem waiting for sex. As a guy, specifically a married guy, you just can't do that. You don't have the time.

• _Pay No Attention To Your Wife._

If you have been married for a while, you are probably not giving your wife enough attention to keep her happy. If she gets angry at you a lot, this is probably the reason. Most marriage counselors and relationship books give the same advice. Pay attention to her needs. And her primary need is for attention.

If you are like most married guys, the last thing you want to do is pay more attention to your wife. More likely, you are considering how you can afford separate residences or at least how you can spend more time apart.

If you start paying more attention to your wife, you may make her happier and your married life more bearable. This is a possible course of action, but it is not one we recommend.

You have only one life. Make it about what *you* want, not what your wife wants. Sure she'll be happier if you give her more attention, *but what's in it for you*?

That's why the scientists at *THE EXPERT'S GUIDES™* recommend a different approach. Stop sleeping with your wife and use the extra energy to start shagging loads of attractive women under 35.

You'll be taking care of number one (yourself) and you'll feel healthier and happier for it.

An added bonus is that if you stop paying attention to your wife she will probably leave you.

• *The EXPERT'S GUIDES™ Poll.*

Our pollsters asked a large group of red blooded American married men which they would prefer to do

(1) • Pay more attention to the wife

OR

(2) • Sleep with a different top fashion model every day

100% of the male respondents picked answer number 2 (unless their wives were watching, then 0% picked answer number 2).

If you agree with these patriotic American males that shagging dozens (yes, even hundreds) of beautiful women sounds like a good plan, this book is for you!

Your wedding ring fits properly if it falls off in the sink when you wash your hands with soap.

CHAPTER III

THE WEDDING RING

The first step in creating a successful marriage is to make sure your wedding ring fits *loosely*. Your wedding ring fits properly if it falls off in the sink every time you wash your hands with soap.

If it doesn't, you need to have your ring resized. Tiffany's will resize Tiffany's wedding bands for free.

There are a few important rules to remember about your wedding ring.

First, wear it whenever you are within twenty-five meters of your wife or her friends or either of your relatives. Twenty-five meters is the maximum distance that a woman with 20-20 vision can spot whether or not you are wearing your ring.

If you don't know how much a meter is, make it a quarter of the length of a football field.

If you get within a quarter of a football field of anyone who talks to your wife or any of your wife's friends, you should also wear your ring.

Otherwise take it off!

Be considerate of your girlfriends. For example, you should not wear your wedding ring while you are having sex with another woman. This is simply good manners.

Wearing a wedding ring while you are cheating on your wife may upset your mistress or girlfriend. Reminding her of your married state is rude and can lead to unintended consequences.

Your girl wants to think you are hers while you are with her.

Constant reminders of your marriage can turn even a relatively sane woman into a slavering Bunny Boiler. So try not to mention your wife to your girlfriends.
The reverse is also true.

"Honey, it's not what you think."

CHAPTER IV

Never Tell Your Wife The Truth About Anything

Some men try to be truthful with their wives about everything except their shagging adventures.

This is a big mistake. If you only lie to your wife occasionally, she will be able to tell and you will inevitably get caught.

Instead, you should lie about everything. Lie gratuitously and continuously. Lie to her about what you had for lunch and the weather during your recent business trip. If you are going to the dentist, say you are going to the dermatologist.

• _Believe Your Own Lies._

When you are lying to your wife, you must believe what you are saying.

Otherwise you will be caught by your wife's built-in lie detector.

If she knows you are lying, you cannot build the trust necessary for a successful marriage.

Also it will make it harder to cheat on her.

Within six months, you should be totally comfortable with lying about your non-existent business trips and your numerous liaisons with other women.

Lying is half the battle.

Train yourself to do it well.

It helps if your wife is a very deep sleeper.

CHAPTER · V

HOW TO SNEAK OUT OF THE HOUSE AT NIGHT

Four circumstances can help you with this important prerequisite for cheating on your wife. Consider yourself fortunate if one is present:

(1) Your wife is addicted to sleeping pills.

(2) Your wife is a very deep sleeper.

(3) You have separate bedrooms and yours is the one nearest the door.

(4) You travel a lot on business.

If none of these conditions exists, try to bring one of them about.

For example, let's say you are a Sanitation Department Employee and don't do much business travel. Tell your wife that you need to start taking business trips once or twice a week. On these nights stay at your friend Fred's house, or if you can afford it, rent a small shagging studio and stay there.

If your wife questions the need for your business trips, on the grounds that you work for the Sanitation Department "and the only garbage you need to pick up is right here in New York," explain that garbage is "a global problem that requires global solutions." Tell her that you are going to conventions in other cities to discuss these "difficult issues" with other concerned "sanitation officials."

Remember she was dumb enough to marry a garbageman. She will believe it.

Once you establish a pattern of being away one or two nights per week you now have free time to carry on shagging, notwithstanding your marriage.

If you already have your own separate bedroom at home, don't get too cocky. You should not entertain hookers and girlfriends at home while your wife is in the house. Even if she is a very deep sleeper, the risks are too high. Remember, you are facing almost certain death if she wakes up while your date is loudly orgasming. And if your wife decides to crawl into bed late at night and discovers that she is suddenly the odd woman out in a threesome, you may have to leave the apartment by a nearby window. Instead be thankful you have your own room. Use it to sneak out at night, not to shag other women at home.

Flowers are your friend, especially the cheap ones.

CHAPTER VI

STAY ON GOOD TERMS WITH YOUR WIFE

To get away with a massive shagging campaign while living with your wife (not to mention children) will require that you stay on relatively good terms with your family.

If you are not getting along with your wife, she will be doubly suspicious when you say you are going out for a quart of milk especially if there is already a fresh quart in the fridge.

• *Shag Her Semi-Annually.*

Staying on good terms with your wife can be exhausting and expensive. It means you will have to shag her occasionally. Try having sex with her at least semi-annually.

• _Do something Nice For Her Every Eleven Days._

A corollary of the 2-3-11 Rule explained in _Shagging for America_ (call her every three days, see her every eleven days, but never two days in a row) is that you should try to do something nice for your wife to show your appreciation at least once every eleven days.

Here are some things you can do to stay on good terms.

(1)   Change a diaper.

(2)   Take out the garbage.

(3)   Bring her a present in a Tiffany's box.

(4)   Flowers (buy the cheap ones).

(5)   Take her out for a nice restaurant meal.

(6)   Pay her credit card bill.

(7)   Make her dinner.

(8)   Tell her she looks great and ask her if she has lost weight.

(9)   Call her mother and have a civil conversation.

(10) Say goodbye when you leave the house instead of just slamming the door.

"How about drinks next Thursday?"

CHAPTER VII

Your Cell Phone, The Adulterer's Tool

The cellular phone represents the greatest technological advance in the field of adultery in the history of the world.

You must have a cell phone.

Through your cell, you can be in instant communication with your girlfriends.

Trips to the corner "for a quart of milk" or "the newspaper" are now a chance to chat up your next conquest, or organize the week's shagging schedule.

Turn it off when you get home. If your wife asks to borrow it, say it is broken or you can't find it.

You do not want her reading through the list of girlfriends in your phone.

• <u>*Caller ID Is A Must.*</u>

Women like to call and hang up if you don't answer. That way they think it doesn't count as having called you.

Wrong. You've got caller ID and you know damned well that she called you eleven times in ten minutes.

• *Cell Phone Or Sex Machine?*

Cell phones can also make great sex toys.

Switch your phone from ring to vibration mode. Place the phone inside your date's vagina (this could involve some explaining).

Go to another phone and call yourself on your cell phone.

You will enjoy the results and she might too.

A wife can work wonders with a little steam.

CHAPTER VIII

NEVER GET MAIL AT HOME

Women have preternatural snooping abilities. Therefore, it is dangerous to get mail at home. Place a standing order with the post office to forward all of your mail to the office.

That way even if one of your girlfriends writes you a threatening letter, you will get it at work.

You must assume that your wife reads all of your mail at home, even if she says she doesn't.

Don't be fooled just because the envelopes do not appear to have been tampered with. Wives can work wonders with a little steam.

"Hi. I'm Sam, er...I mean Bob."

CHAPTER IX

ALWAYS CHEAT ON YOUR WIFE UNDER AN ASSUMED NAME

To reduce the risks of getting caught, it is a good idea to do your shagging under an assumed name. Pick something simple for your "nom de shag." "Andrew" or "Bob" will do just fine. Call yourself "Casanova" or "Shag Man" and everyone will see you coming a mile away.

Have business cards printed up in your shagging name. List the address of your shagging studio if you have one. Otherwise your cell phone number will suffice. Hand these out to potential conquests, but keep your home and work numbers to yourself.

If you successfully pull off your new secret identity, you will be able to cheat on your wife with impunity.

Having a "nom de shag" will leave your girlfriends and mistresses unable to retaliate against your marriage.

On the other hand, if you do get caught shagging under an assumed name, it looks worse than if you had done it openly, because it is so obviously premeditated.

A shagging name should be used only with total strangers, not women who know or could easily find out who you really are.

For example, don't try it with your wife's friends.

Borrow a kid and a dog.

CHAPTER • X

USE YOUR MARRIED STATE AS A GIRL MAGNET

One of the best aphrodisiacs for most women is a handsome guy with a small child (under 3 years old) walking a beautiful dog or puppy in the park.

With the dog and the kid, you are conveying the warmth and security that she is looking for.

If you can take care of a kid and a dog it is a good bet you can take care of her.

If you don't have a kid or a dog, borrow them from friends. They will be delighted to have you take them off their hands for an hour or two. This is much better then using your own children who can rat you out to your wife, if they are old enough to talk.

Take your borrowed charges to Central Park and watch what happens. Girls will run up to you to ask you about the kid and the dog. Be responsive and warm and let her play with your companions.

Since you won't be wearing your wedding ring, you can tell each woman about your painful divorce. Since women are inherently competitive and aware of how evil other women can be, your targets should be very sympathetic.

When you've gotten enough phone numbers, return your charges to their rightful owners and go home and watch a football game.

Forget about working out.

CHAPTER XI

DON'T TRY TO LOOK BETTER

You don't need to look good. You're a guy.

Don't waste your time working out. It will make you feel lousy to stand next to all the male models in the gym. And it's exhausting.

Face it. You're a short, scrawny, pot-bellied, balding bastard. Worse yet, you are married.

But you have one big advantage.

You are mean.

• *<u>Be Charismatic Instead.</u>*

Practice saying "Hello, darling" in the same voice as Cary Grant.

Affect an easy careless attitude. Smile all the time. Pretend to listen to what she says. Act engaged in the conversation.

Practice your facial expressions in the mirror.

Learn how to raise an eyebrow like Clint Eastwood in *For a Few Dollars More.*

When you find an attractive facial expression, fix your features and don't move them as you go through the motions of seducing your date.

Concentrating on this will help you keep your mouth shut.

You are a toxic husband.

CHAPTER · XII

SHAGGERS DON'T BOND

Born shaggers don't bond. Getting emotionally attached is not our thing. We aren't going to be happy with just one woman.

Every woman you would consider sleeping with probably has something wonderful to offer. But there is no reason to get bogged down in it.

Instead, present all the signs of emotional involvement. Give her flowers, tell her you are crazy about her, take her to great parties and on wonderful short vacations. Make passionate love to her. Then, when the novelty wears off or it looks like you might get caught, don't return any of her phone calls.

Women will call you damaged.

They will whisper that you are a toxic bachelor.

It doesn't matter. They are wrong. You are not a toxic bachelor.

You are a toxic *husband*.

• _Shagging And Bragging._

You should not shag and brag. Be discrete about your girlfriends. For example, never mention your girlfriends to the media.

Tell only your closest male friends. Don't worry. They will let everyone else know what a great shagger you are.

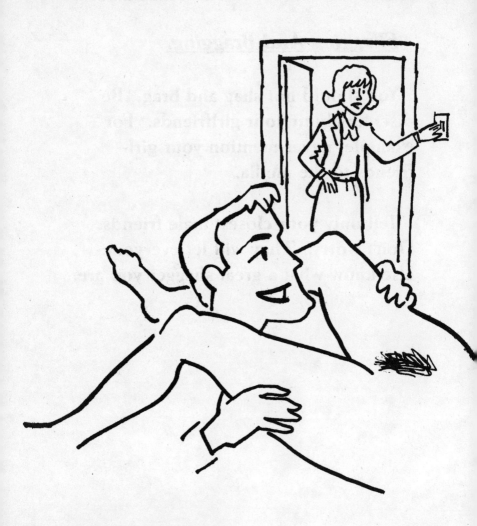

Eating is not cheating.

CHAPTER • XIII

EATING IS NOT CHEATING

Adultery can get you into big trouble in a subsequent divorce action. It is also illegal in many jurisdictions. It is therefore important to understand the technical issues involved in defining adultery so that you can lie effectively about the facts later.

Adultery comes from the concept of adulterating which mean adding impurities. Thus adultery can be defined as mixing your genital fluids with hers. The biological basis for this definition is the instinctive male desire to know that his children are actually the result of adding his sperm to the stew and not those of some other male.

This narrower definition of adultery which is now generally accepted by former President Clinton and other great shaggers everywhere, substantially reduces the number of situations which can give rise to adultery.

Under this definition, eating is not cheating. Neither is anal sex. In fact, anything short of full sexual intercourse where you come inside her cannot be adultery.

And, if you wear a condom, even this is not adultery, since (unless the condom breaks) you have not adulterated her precious bodily fluids with yours.

Stick to this definition when accused by your wife of cheating. Under this approach, which was endorsed by former President Clinton in his testimony about his relationship with Monica Lewinsky, it is very unlikely that you have committed adultery.

At worst, you may have engaged in "inappropriate behavior."

"Let's talk about it later."

CHAPTER XIV

DEALING WITH THE ULTIMATUM

Women have a time limit. They hit the wall at 35. Your girl will want to set a time limit for you. This time limit is called *The Ultimatum*.

The Ultimatum is the time by which you must:

(a) leave your wife and/or
(b) marry your girlfriend.

Eventually your mistress or girlfriend will give you *The Ultimatum*:

"Leave your wife and marry me by the first of next year or you're history!"

Don't kid yourself. She means it. And she is not going to forget about it. *The Ultimatum* means it's time for evasive action.

• _Evasive Action._

Here are some suggestions when she gives you _The Ultimatum._

(1)   Change the subject and say "We'll talk about it later."

(2)   Buy her jewelry or a new pair of shoes.

(3)   Look at your feet and say nothing. Then:

   (i) slowly keel over and fall to the floor, or
  (ii) clutch your stomach and start screaming in pain.

(4)   Tell her you love her and beg for another six months of meaningless sex.

(5)   Tell her you'll do it just as soon as the kids are off to college.

(6)   Tell her you need a few more months of careful planning with your divorce lawyer.

(7)   Tell her you'll do it just as soon as you can get your wife out of your house.

(8)   Say you just need to find a more secure job first.

(9)   Tell her you will do it as soon as you recover from your last divorce.

(10) Move to London.

Another foolproof method is to tell her that you will make a decision in six months, except that every time she brings up the subject, this deadline is automatically extended for another two weeks. Don't worry. The deadline will never arrive. In fact, it will keep getting farther away. That's because she is biologically incapabable of keeping quiet on this subject.

Try sleeping with attractive women.

CHAPTER XV

IMPOTENCE AND WHAT TO DO ABOUT IT

Impotence is a myth made up by ugly women. There is actually no such thing. But if you feel you have it, the best cure is to get divorced or change girlfriends.

Then try sleeping with *attractive* women.

If you must sleep with ugly women, here's a helpful tip:

Don't look at your girlfriend during sex.

This will ruin your concentration.

Keep your eyes closed and think of the things that make you come in a minute or less when you are masturbating.

This will keep you focused.

If impotence is still a problem, there are three possibilities:

(1)   You are gay,
or

(2)   You have a medical problem (in which case, see a doctor), or

(3)   You are trying to have sex with your wife.

If you like to dress up like Elton John...

CHAPTER XVI

HOW TO TELL IF YOU ARE GAY

Visit an adult bookstore and go to the gay section. Look through a few magazines.

If you feel a stiffy coming on, you are gay.

If you like to dress up like Elton John or if you find that most of your dates have big hands and feet and large Adam's apples, you are gay.

George Michael albums in your CD collection are another bad sign.

If images of firm male bottoms keep invading your thoughts, you are either gay or a woman trapped in a man's body.

In either case, this book is not for you.

Save your socks. And shag more women.

CHAPTER XVII

TIME IS PUSSY

• *She Has A Different Relationship To Time.*

Men and women don't have the same sense of time.

One semi-smart businessman started a "hurry-dating" service where all the men and women would meet in a big room. Each woman would spend five minutes with each man for a mutual introduction. The idea was that at the end, each person could ask out the girl or guy they like best.

It didn't work.

The women said five minutes wasn't long enough to get to know anyone.

The guys said, "What do I do with the other four minutes?"

• *Get In And Out Quickly.*

Every woman has something wonderful to offer and some women have many wonderful qualities.

The main thing you need to know about this is that you do not have to marry her or even spend a lot of time or money on her to get these things.

The trick is to get her to willingly give of herself without getting yourself entangled in the tentacles of a long-term relationship.

To do this, you've got to learn to get in and get out quickly.

He who shags and runs away will live to shag another day.

• _She Wants To Know Why You Like Her._

A woman who is interested in you will be very curious what you like about her. Ther's because she wants to feel special.

Be prepared to lie.

She does not want to hear (to paraphrase a recent American president):

"It's the _pussy_, stupid!"

• *Study Anatomy.*

To be a great shagger, it is sometimes helpful to have at least a cursory knowledge of anatomy.

Many of you have asked, "What's that fleshy part around the vagina?"

This is easy. It's the woman!

• _Masturbation._

Men often ask what they should masturbate into.

The answer is that a woman is just as good as an old sock.

In a pinch, even your wife will do.

So save your socks and shag more women.

"I like my $500,000 a year job, get along with my parents, my last relationship was for more than five years and I fell in love with you at first sight."

CHAPTER · XVIII

HOW TO ACCELERATE HER SHAG-BY-DATE

As a married man, you have limited time for your shagging campaign.

It may take several encounters and numerous phone calls with a woman before you get her into bed.

Since you don't have as much time as a single guy, you should use these "shag-by-date accelerators" to get her into bed more quickly.

• _Answers To Frequently Asked Questions From Your Date._

Most women look for certain things in men. Emotional and financial health, ability to bond with others, love of children and animals, respect for women and, of course, good looks, money, fame, power, intelligence, charisma and important real estate holdings. As a reader of this book, the chances are you don't have any of these things. As a result, you will have to pick a few to lie about.

Here are some suggestions.

• _Emotional Health And Ability To Bond._

In the first few dates, a woman will always ask you the following questions:

• _Do You Like Your Job?_

There is only one correct answer: an unqualified yes.

If you don't like your job, it shows you are not effective in getting what you want and she won't want to be with you. After all, if you have a job you don't want, you might marry a woman you don't want.

Even if you are a cesspool cleaner, tell her you love your work.

• *Do You Get Along Well With Your Parents?*

Again, there is only one correct answer: yes. Women instinctively know that their relationship with you will mirror your relationship with your parents.

If you have an angry or stormy relationship with your mother, she knows that you are going to have problems in relating to women. Instead of admitting that the mere sight of your mother makes you apoplectic, tell your date how you enjoy taking your mom for long walks and how you pay for her to go to Florida for a nice vacation once a year. But don't get carried away. For example, never admit that you still live with your mother.

• _What Was Your Longest Relationship With a Woman?_

The correct answer is "more than five years." This will put her mind at rest because it shows you are capable of a serious sustained relationship. It helps to say you lived together for at least four of the five years. Women are in it for the long haul.

It is a bad idea to admit that, as is likely the case, you have never sustained a relationship that lasted longer than a moderately severe cold.

• _Do You Own Your House Or Apartment Or Rent It?_

The correct answer is you own it. If she asks, you also own your house in the Hamptons (even if you don't have one). And you would never consider being in a share house. These answers show your long term financial stability. Never mind that they aren't true.

Try to convey all this information quickly, at the beginning of the first date. Then make the big push to get her up to your shagging studio or hotel room.

• _Are You Married?_

The correct answer is "no". If you feel you must tell the truth about this, have your head examined first. If you must admit you are married say you are finalizing your divorce and things "should be wrapped up in six months or so."

• _Tell Her It Was Love At First Sight._

Tell every woman you date that you knew she was the one the instant you saw her for the first time. Tell her it was love at first sight. Tell her she is your soulmate. This is extremely effective because she has likely been waiting for her whole life to hear this.

If it turns out to be true, she will remember this, treasure it and talk about it for the rest of her life. If, as is more likely, it turns out not to be true, you will at least get her into bed more quickly.

The more passionate you are, the more open she will be. The more you tell her you love her, the more she will like you and the quicker you will get her breasts out.

Have sex with complete strangers.

CHAPTER XIX

NEVER HAVE SEX WITH ANYONE YOU KNOW

Since you are married, you already know that there are very good reasons to be afraid of intimacy.

For one thing: *it's boring.*

Having sex with someone you know is like masturbating with your mother in the room. If it happens, it's a miracle.

Let's face it, sex is embarrassing. That's why you should only have it with complete strangers. Preferably two female strangers.

If you can't find any strangers, you may be reduced to sleeping with your wife's friends.

Your wife's friends aren't getting any either.

CHAPTER XX

SLEEPING WITH YOUR WIFE'S FRIENDS

As a married man, you may not have unfettered access to attractive women. Most likely your wife has dragged you out to live in the suburbs to keep you away from all those gorgeous city girls. And your women friends will not be anxious to set you up on dates. In short, you feel isolated.

Don't despair. Your wife is bound to have female friends. They may even live close by. And since many of them are probably married, you know they aren't getting any either.

Start building your harem using your wife's friends or your friends' wives. There is no group of women more desperate for sex than married women. They are gagging for it and they have the same need for secrecy as you do.

Personal ads are for one reason only: to help married men get laid.

CHAPTER • XXI

MAKE EFFECTIVE USE OF PERSONAL ADS

Personal ads are for one purpose only. To allow married men to get laid more quickly.

Don't look for a relationship in the lonely hearts pages. These women are desperate. And that's what we like about them.

Go straight to the category that you are really interested in: *attached seeking a discreet encounter.*

If nothing seems appetizing, skim the *women seeking men* selections. Eliminate the ones that mention the words "marriage," "children," "long-term committed relationship," "take it slow" or "serious monogamous relationship."

Now that you have eliminated all the ads taken out by women, you will be left with the remaining ads. These ads are all taken out by transvestites and hookers.

Now go back and reread the ads you previously eliminated. Pick the ones you like and respond to them under a "nom de shag," carefully sprinkling the words "marriage," "relationship," "serious," "unattached," "financially secure," "generous" and "monogamous" throughout your answer.

Also use the words "huge" or "enormous" as appropriate.

Then make sure your bachelor pad is available.

Your phone will be ringing off the hook within several days.

"Hookers should be cheap and grateful."

CHAPTER • XXII

HOOKERS ARE
A NECESSITY

What can you say about hookers? A few words come to mind. "Fantastic!", "unbelievable!", "right-on!" and "God's greatest gift to mankind!"

Hookers should have six principal qualities. They should be:

(1) Beautiful,

(2) Young (but legal),

(3) Cheap,

(4) Unable to speak English,

(5) Available by phone, and

(6) Grateful for your patronage.

Without hookers, life would be very bleak for the married man. The best place to find hookers is on business trips to third world countries. In New York and London, they are just too expensive.

Try to get a job that involves travel to emerging markets. Russia, Cuba, Eastern Europe, and almost any non-Muslim country in South East Asia are your best bets.

The presence of lovely, cheap and grateful women in these countries is overwhelming.

There are just three rules for dealing with these women:

(1)   Don't ever get involved with them. Keep it a strictly professional relationship.

(2)   Wear a bag.

(3)   Don't reveal your name or address.

Hookers are no mess and no fuss. Use them liberally.

Don't have sex in front of your enemies.

CHAPTER • XXIII

WIFE SWAPPING

If your wife won't let you out of the house and has no attractive girlfriends, you can always suggest wife swapping. This last resort for bored suburban couples can be stressful as well as fun. Unfortunately, wife swapping may mean having sex with another man's wife while your wife is watching.

It is much more satisfying to have sex with another man's wife while your wife is not watching. And there is always the danger that your partner's husband will be nearby and will also be watching. This means you may have two potentially mortal enemies in the room with you while you are trying to have sex. Some men report that this interferes with their concentration.

As a general rule, we do not recommend wife swapping. You are better off not involving your wife when you are trying to cheat on her. It's just too complicated.

Don't offend your wife by cheating on her with older women.

ALWAYS SLEEP WITH WOMEN WHO ARE YOUNGER THAN YOUR WIFE

If you are married and reading this book, your wife is probably over 35. This is a problem.

Women are like flowers. And who wants a bunch of old flowers? It is unsportsmanlike to sleep with women who are past their sell-by date.

Don't make matters worse by cheating on your wife with other women who are also over 35. This will be doubly humiliating for your wife. She will understand it if you cheat on her with a younger woman. If you commit adultery on her with an older woman, your wife will be crushed.

Have some respect for your wife. Make sure all your mistresses are younger than she is.

"Do you have something in a tall affluent bisexual blond?"

TRADING UP

The time comes in the marriage of every successful man when he will want to trade up. So try not to get too attached to your wife.

You know it's time to trade up when:

(1)   Your mother starts taking her side in arguments.

(2)   She develops varicose veins.

(3) She starts making major credit card purchases without telling you.

(4) Her age plus her weight is a number greater than 165.

(5) Her CSM ratio (the ratio of cellulite and stretch marks to the surface area of her skin) exceeds 5%.

(6) She insists on having sex with you without another woman being present.

(7) She is not blond and is either:
(i) under 5'9" tall or
(ii) not bisexual.

(8) She is over 35.

(9) She:
   (i) contracts a potentially fatal illness, and
   (ii) is not rich.

(10) She sleeps with all your friends and you don't care.

Clandestinely record your wife's every move.

PREPARE FOR DIVORCE NOW

Don't wait. Get divorced now! But be prepared. Divorce is very expensive.

A divorce will generally cost you at least 250% of what your wife's family spent on the wedding.

If your wedding cost them $100,000, your divorce will cost you $250,000.

There is a very good reason why divorce is so expensive.

It's worth it.

If you are mounting a massive campaign of adultery, you must be prepared in case you get caught.

If your wife catches you unprepared and in bed with her best friend (or yours), you could be facing an expensive court battle.

You can take effective steps now to reduce the cost of a possible divorce. As with many other things, in divorce, preparation is 90% of the battle.

Here are five positive steps you can take now to prepare for your divorce:

(1)   Carry around a portable tape recorder. Turn it on whenever she yells or throws things at you.

(2)   Limit the amount of cash in your joint account. Cancel any overdraft facility on this account. Don't put her name on your credit cards and keep all real estate and leases in your own name. Put her car lease in her name.

(3)   Use your cell phone for all
       shagging activities (that's what
       it's for!). Put a recording
       device on your phone at work
       so when she yells at you in the
       office, you will have it on tape.

(4)   Get her to sign a post-nuptial
       agreement. This won't be easy.
       You may have to bribe your
       wife to sign (a new car, lots of
       cash, maybe some plastic
       surgery).

(5)   Negotiate with a storage com-
       pany for space to store her
       stuff. If she won't go peaceful-
       ly, you may have to move her
       things into storage on very
       short notice.

In divorce, as in war, the stakes are too high to take chances. You must think of everything she could conceivably use against you. If you don't, rest assured that she will.

Immediately throw out or move to a safe place your pornography collection, videos and pictures of you having sex with other women, incriminating correspondence and sex toys. Keep in mind that anything that can conceivably be used against you will be.

Try to take the offensive by photographing her in incriminating positions. Keep the pictures in a safe place. Collect all the dirt you can from her ex-girlfriends and boyfriends.

If you have been married to her for more than a very short time, you should easily be able to think of something compromising that she did that you can use against her.

With any luck, the villagers will do the rest.

CHAPTER · XXVI

How To Get Rid Of Your Wife

Once you are prepared for your divorce, you can be sure that the time will come when you can no longer stand being around your wife even for short periods of time.

You know it's time to get rid of your wife when:

(1) You start getting up two hours earlier so you can be the first one at work.

(2) You feel a wave of anger when you come home from work and she says "Hello," and she feels the same way when you say "Hello."

(3) When she starts throwing kitchen appliances at you before you even have a chance to point out what a bitch she is.

(4)   When you can't wait to get away on your next business trip.

(5)   When the only time you have sex with your wife is after a violent quarrel.

Fortunately, scientists have come up with a number of clever solutions to the world's oldest problem: how to get rid of your wife.

Here are ten of them:

(1)   Take her on a romantic tour of the rural areas of Libya, Iran or Iraq. Go to the public square and stand near a pile of stones, then loudly accuse her of adultery in Arabic. With any luck, the villagers will do the rest.

(2)   Let half a dozen mice loose in the apartment just before you go on a long business trip.

(3) **Stop talking to your wife and ignore her completely, particularly when she is speaking to you or asking you a direct question.**

(4) **Cut off all her credit cards and stop giving her money.**

(5) **Tell her you contracted herpes from her best friend.**

(6) **Tell her that you have been gay for as long as you can remember.**

(7) **Tell her you lost your job and she will have to go back to work to support both of you.**

(8) **Leave a used condom conspicuously in the bedroom garbage can and a pair of tacky woman's crotchless panties under the covers in the bed.**

(9) **Tell her repeatedly that you "hadn't realized she was so fat."**

(10) **Pretend to be sexually attracted to her dog.**

When you are in love, don't sign anything.

CHAPTER XXVIII

THE BEST TIME TO GET MARRIED IS NEVER

• *There Is No Such Thing As A Good Reason To Get Married.*

People get married for many reasons. None of them good.

Here are the five reasons people cite when they get married:

(1) For love

(2) For money

(3) For children

(4) For sex

(5) Because their dog or cat died

All of these are actually reasons to stay single!

• *Love Is A Delusional State.*

Love is one of the most dangerous mental illnesses that most human beings will face in their lifetime.

People who are in love often do strange and irrational things like get married or put their property in some-one else's name.

When in love, you may not be respon-sible for your actions. Never-theless, you will have to take the conse-quences. So be very careful.

Whatever you do, when you're in love, don't sign anything!

If you find yourself falling in love, call an escort service and order up a couple of hookers. A threesome will help you put things in perspective.

Fortunately, love rarely lasts very long, although, in severe cases it can linger on for a year or more.

Most cases of love are quickly cured by six months of marriage. Married or not and however long it takes, one day you will wake up and realize that you now have a strange person living in your house who has your happiness in her hands. And you may suddenly find that you do not know this person. You may find that you don't even like her.

And yes, you are in big trouble.

Love is a great reason to get naked. It is not a reason to get married. It might also be a reason to lock yourself in an igloo at the North Pole until it passes.

• _Don't Marry For Money._

If you marry for money, you will earn every penny of it.

Marrying the rich involves enormous self sacrifice. Unless you are the kind of person who enjoys subordinating his own needs and desires to someone else, don't attempt it.

If you marry a much wealthier person, they will have the power, not you. Enjoying the luxuries will mean doing what your spouse wants when she wants it.

And if you stop playing the game, the rich have the resources to discard you like an old dog.

Marrying the rich is not for the faint-hearted.

• _Sex._

Sex is not a reason to get married. The longer you are married the less sex you will have. After six months, it may cease altogether.

Besides who wants to have sex over and over with the same person?

Sex is the single best reason I know to stay single.

• _Children._

Children are also not a reason to get married.

While many American women are hung up on the idea that you should be married to have children, most European women don't feel that way.

Try having children with a Scandinavian girl. They generally won't insist on marriage. Anyway they are much better looking than Americans.

If you do get married to have children, you still have a better than 50% chance of getting divorced. If you stay single and have children, you can guarantee that you will avoid the heartbreak and expense of divorce.

• *Your Dog Or Cat Died.*

This is also not a reason to get married. Instead, just buy a new dog or cat. This will save you hundreds of thousands of dollars.

The secret of any successful marriage is divorce.

CHAPTER XXIX

The Twenty Secrets Of A Successful Marriage

(1)   Make sure your wedding ring fits loosely.

(2)   Never tell your wife the truth about anything.

(3)   Always cheat on your wife under an assumed name.

(4)   There is no sex after marriage (at least with your wife).

(5)   Never cheat on your wife with a woman who is older than she is.

(6)   Marriage need not be a life sentence.

(7)   The secret of any successful marriage is divorce.

(8)   Eating is not cheating.

(9)   Stay on good terms with your wife until you trade her in.

(10) Beware of wife swapping.

(11) Use your cellphone-the adulterer's tool.

(12) Take lots of "business trips."

(13) Rent a bachelor's pad.

(14) Intimacy is a bore.

(15) Familiarity breeds divorce.

(16) Tell all your mistresses it was love at first sight.

(17) Never give out your home
       phone number.

(18) Never get mail at home.

(19) Remember that time is pussy.

(20) He who shags and runs away
       will live to shag another day.

Adulterers be proud!

You are cheating for America.

The best damned country in the World!

130

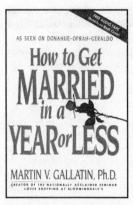

HOW TO GET MARRIED IN A YEAR OF LESS
by Dr. M. Gallatin

Have we got a book for you! These strategies are literally guaranteed to work–or your money back! Author was featured on *Oprah* and in *The NY Times*. These well thought out tips, tactics & techniques also tell you where to go to meet the right people, and how to act when you do! A great gift for both men and women, young and old!

Retail Price: $17.95 • Special Price: $16.95

Cloth • 6" x 9" • 276 pgs • Illustrations • ISBN: 1-56171-980-3

THE JOY OF DEPPRESSION
by David Rudnitsky, M.D.

A hilarious comic send-up of all the popular self-help guides. Author is a noted neurotic, who humorously covers every aspect of being depressed.

Packed with outrageous illustrations.

Retail Price: $4.99 • Special Price: $3.99

Soft • 4" x 7" • 192 pgs • Illus. • ISBN: 1-56171-273-6

IS HE FOR REAL?: *Knowing Sooner What A Man Will Be Like Later*
by David Samson & Elayne J. Kahn, Ph.D.

This powerful guide, pached with intimate details, finally gives women the upper hand in deciding who's Mr Right–and definitely who's Mr. Wrong! Written by a comedian and a Harvard Ph.D., the authors get to the heart of understanding men's "Secret Signals Of Romance". Read this book and you are guaranteed to learn how to decipher all of his hidden Love Codes!

Retail Price: $12.95 • Special Price: $11.95

Hard • 6" x 6" • 160 pgs • ISBN: 1-56171-985-4

THE FUNNIEST MAN IN THE WORLD: *The Wild and Crazy Humor of Ephraim Kishon* • by Ephraim Kishon

This book contain hilarious stories full of life's everyday characters by Israel's most famous humorist–who also happens to be the World's bestselling humor writer with 64 million books sold in 50 languages! These are the best and funniest stories culled from the author's past 25 books.
For Ages 10 to Adult.

Retail Price: $12.95 • Special Price: $11.95

Cloth • 6" x 9" • 224 pgs • ISBN: 0-944007-47-3

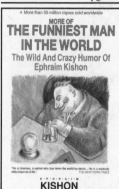

MORE OF THE FUNNIEST MAN IN THE WORLD: *The Wild and Crazy Humor of Ephraim Kishon* by Ephraim Kishon

This book contains more hilarious stories full of life's everyday characters by Israel's most famous humorist–who also happens to be the World's bestselling humor writer with 64 million books sold in 50 languages! These are more of the best and funniest stories culled from the author's past 25 books.
For Ages 10 to Adult.

Retail Price: $12.95 • Special Price: $11.95

Cloth • 6" x 9" • 200 pgs • ISBN: 0-944007-48-1

DO REALITY CHECKS EVER BOUNCE?: *And 121 Other Questions Too Big To Answer!* • by David Samson

A book that doesn't pretend to have answers, only the funniest and most strangely profound questions you could have ever imagined.

Each question is an ideal conversation opener, perfect for parties and gatherings.
There is no end to the hilarity! Samples include:
• Do suicide notes wind up in dead letter files?
• Would dyslexic people see evain as naive?

Retail Price: $9.95 • Special Price: $8.95

Hard • 7" x 7" • 128 pgs • ISBN: 1-56171-998-6

THE BAD WORDS DICTIONARY
by Voy Sobon

Europe's best-selling *Bad Words Dictionary* has taken the U.S. market by storm! "You cheap son of a *kutwijf*," the taxi driver snarls. "What kind of *geodkoop* tip is that?" "You *cheekoosho* piece of *kooso*", the rude witer shouts, embarrassing you in front of your friends. How do you respond? Get this book and you'll always be ready! With the *Bad Words Dictionary*, you'll never be at loss for the proper off-color response.

Retail Price: $7.95 • Special Price: $6.95

Paper • 4.5" x 7.5" • 304 pgs • ISBN: 1-56171-175-6

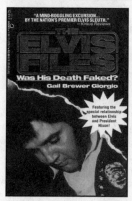

THE ELVIS FILES
by Gail Brewer-Giorgio

The world's leading Elvis sleuth author of a previous *New York Times* Bestseller on Elvis, presents the facts, intrigues, and provocative unsolved questions surrounding the mysterious "death" of the King.

Retail Price: $4.99 • Special Price: $3.99

Paper • 4 1/2" x 7" • 288 pgs • ISBN: 1-56171-376-7

WATCH YOUR CLEAVAGE, CHECK YOUR ZIPPER • by Guy LeBow

TV veteran Guy LeBow takes you on a hilarious romp through the early days of television! LeBow's insider stories of boob tube lore will introduce you to the side of television you never saw on the screen...Catch what happens when: A performer spills hot soup on Lebow's crotch over live national TV! The romantic leading man in a TV drama gets double exposure by leaving his fly wide open. A chesty advertiser accidentally shows too much of her wares. Wrestlers stuff socks in their jocks. "...juicy!" –*Cindy Adams, New York Post*

Retail Price: $5.99 • Special Price: $4.99

Paper • 4" x 7" • 315 pgs • ISBN: 1-56171-284-1

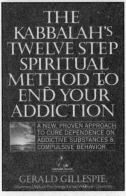

THE KABBALAH'S 12-STEP SPIRITU-AL METHOD TO END YOUR ADDICTION: *A New Proven Approach To Cure Dependence On Addictive Substances & Compulsive Behaviors* • by Gerald Gillespie

This book combines centuries of ancient wisdom with 12-step recovery methods. Kabbalah, the Biblical Jewish mystical and meditative tradition, is not merely a philosophy but a way of life. Kabbalah can be one's roadmap to spiritual recovery as well as physical recovery from addictive behaviors or substances that are limiting or threatening one's well being.

Retail Price: $18.95 • Special Price: $17.95

Trade Paper • 6" x 9" • 256 pgs • ISBN: 1-56171-960-9

YOU CAN BE DRIVEN SANE: *Know Yourself & Heal Yourself–A Journey Of Self Discovery*
by Dr. Simon Speyer

This world-renowned Dutch psychotherapist uses elements of holistic health science, nueropsychology, and even computer science to help readers toward a greater understanding of themselves and their behavior. Only minutes a day will help readers confront and conquer their problems.

Retail Price: $5.50 • Special Price: $4.99

Soft • 4" x 7" • 226 pgs • ISBN: 1-56171-337-6

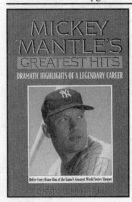

MICKEY MANTLE'S GREATEST HITS • by David S. Nuttall

This book takes readers back to majestic Yankee Stadium and other classic ball parks of the Fifties & Sixties. Coming to the plate, amid rising anitcipation in the hearts of thousands of fans, is the handsome "kid from Oklahoma". The grace and power of this remarkable athlete comes alive as you follow the game details of each vital "at bat" that contributed to his legend.

Retail Price: $14.95 • Special Price: $13.95

Paper • 4.5" x 7.5" • 304 pgs • Photos • ISBN: 1-56171-175-6

THE ART OF THE SHMOOZE:
A Savvy Social Guide for Getting to the Top • by Bret Saxon & Steve Stein

From the bestselling authors of the definitive book on meeting celebrities (How To Meet & Hang Out With the Stars) comes this ambitious, sophisticated guide to approaching and establishing rapport with anyone in a superior position. The fawning deference and awe that we were always taught to show higher-ups only boomerangs in one's face today. This is the ultimate book for business networking.

Retail Price: $21.95 • Special Price: $19.95

Paper • 4.5" x 7.5" • 304 pgs • Photos • ISBN: 1-56171-175-6

HELP YOURSELF TO HAPPINESS:
See Yourself In A Whole New Way
by Gerald Jackson

What's holding you back? If you are one of the very few who has mastered the art of living, then put down this book! However, if you are still looking for the secrets of happiness, health, and prosperous living, then read on, because this book was written for you!

Retail Price: $5.50 • Special Price: $4.99

Cloth • 4" x 7" • 260 pgs • ISBN: 1-56171-314-4

THE ART OF CLOSING ANY DEAL:
How To Be A "Master Closer" In Everything You Do • by Jim Pickens

Over 1 million copies sold–perfect for entrepreneurs, executives, and anyone who works in sales and marketing and wants to improve their crucial "closing" and selling skills. Endorsed by the Chairman of IBM and by Sam Walton, founder of Wal Mart.

Retail Price: $18.95 • Special Price: $17.95

Cloth • 6" x 9" • 276 pgs • ISBN: 1-56171-175-6

PRINCESS DIANA: *The Hidden Evidence*
by Jon King & John Beveridge

Was Princess Diana murdered? Or was she the victim of an innocent though tragic accident? If she was murdered, who did it? Who ordered the killing and what were the motives behind it?

Based on information received from a veteran CIA contract agent one week prior to the crash in Paris–plus further evidence obtained from other highly placed sources, this investigative work presents an uncompromising inquiry into Diana's death.

This thoroughly researched book reveals the shocking truth behind the most scandalous, closely guarded secret in the UK's history.

Retail Price: $24.95 • Special Price: $23.95

Hard • 6" x 9" • 432 pgs • ISBN: 1-56171-922-6

THE MARILYN FILES
by Robert Slatzer

This definitive story of Marilyn's murder will shock you. Contains personal details from Monroe's ex-husbend, author Bob Slatzer, who maintained a close relationship throughout her life. Provides an exhaustive and well-researched analysis of all the circumstances surrounding Marilyn's death. Reveals a wide variety of scenarios, identifies all the possible suspects including RFK and even JFK. With expert testimony to back it up, the book calls for a reopening of the murder case.

Retail Price: $5.99 • Special Price: $4.99

Soft • 4" x 7" • 314 pgs • ISBN: 1-56171-147-0

HOLLYWOOD'S UNSOLVED MYSTERIES • by John Austin

Here is a compelling exposé of Hollywood's most sinister true-crime cases. A great source of information about Marilyn Monroe, her murder, the Kennedys, Peter Lawford and more. Also goes into detail about William Holden, Bob Crane, Natalie Wood and others. Learn how greed, lust and envy drove celebrities to untimely deaths. "Move over, *Hollywood Babylon*! Something here for every film fan." –*Los Angeles Daily News*

Retail Price: $5.99 • Special Price: $4.99

Soft • 4" x 7" • 273 pgs • ISBN: 1-56171-065-2

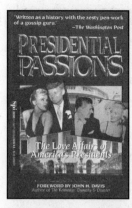

PRESIDENTIAL PASSIONS: *The Love Affairs of America's Presidents*
by Michael John Sullivan

"Sullivan comes up with fascinating new details."–*New York Newsday*. Another source of information about Marilyn, her untimely death, JFK, Reagan, and other talented Cassanova U.S. Presidents! This colorful collection will surprise and shock you–but the stories are all verifiable true. "History class was never like this. Now we know where Washington *really* slept"–*New York Daily News*

Retail Price: $5.95 • Special Price: $4.95

Soft • 4" x 7" • 289 pgs • ISBN: 1-56171-093-8

SWEETHEARTS OF '60s TV
by L. Smith

The inspiring, heartwarming and surprising stories of the girls America tuned-in to watch every week in the 60's. These glamorous and sexy stars made the 1960's a "time to remember". Features Goldie Hawn, Jude Carne, Sally Field, Barbara Eden and many more.

Retail Price: $5.50 • Special Price: $4.99

Cloth • 4" x 7" • 224 pgs • ISBN: 1-56171-206-X

HOLLYWOOD'S GREATEST MYSTERIES • by John Austin

Hollywood columnist and author John Austin takes the reader well beyond the prepared and doctored statements of studio publicists to expose omissions and contradictions in police and coroner's reports. The author proves that we have not been told the truth about the deaths of Elvis Presley, Marilyn Monroe, Jean Harlow and others.

Retail Price: $5.99 • Special Price: $4.99

Soft • 4" x 7" • 288 pgs • Photos • ISBN: 1-56171-258-2

THE MAFIA, CIA AND GEORGE BUSH: *The Untold Story Of America's Greatest Financial Debacle*
by P. Brewton

If you thought the S&L scandal rocked the Bush administration, you've got to read what this investigative journalist has uncovered about the former president, a circle of Texas cronies and billionaries, the Mafia and covert CIA assistance. The U.S. taxpayers lose out to the tune of half a trillion dollors, while the criminals go free and get richer!

Retail Price: $23.95 • Special Price: $19.95

Hard • 6" x 9" • 420 pgs • Photos • ISBN: 1-56171-203-5

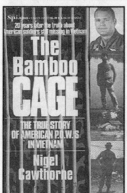

THE BAMBOO CAGE: *The True Story Of American P.O.W.s In Vietnam*
by Nigel Cawthorne

The government claims that over 2,000 American soldiers missing-in-action in the Vietnam War are dead. The author, a respected British researcher and published writer of more than 50 books, fought for crucial information and documentation from the CIA, the Pentagon and even the authorities in Hanoi to prove otherwise. Revealed here are the cruel and illegal secrets that the U.S. government doesn't want you to ever know.

Retail Price: $5.95 • Special Price: $4.95

Paper • 4" x 7" • 366 pgs • Photos • ISBN: 1-56171-241-8

TARGET AMERICA: *Terrorism In The World Today* • by Y. Bodansky

Can we breathe easier now that the Government has beefed up its counter–terrorism capabilities? Not according to the Director of the U.S. Congress's Task Force on Terrorism & Unconventional Warfare. Terrorist groups from Islamic and Balkan countries are primed to strike both in Europe and in the U.S. This book reveals much previously unknown information on these dangerous murderous criminals.

Retail Price: $5.99 • Special Price: $4.99

Paper • 4" x 7" • 315 pgs • Photos • ISBN: 1-56171-269-8

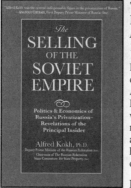

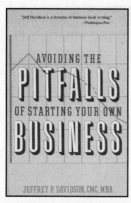

AVOIDING THE PITFALLS OF STARTING YOUR OWN BUSINESS
by Jeferey Davidson

Nine out of ten new businesses don't last long enough to become old ones. Too many entrepreneurs make highly avoidable errors–and then lose their life savings, their friends, marriages, and their self-respect. Whether you are contemplating a new business or you want to know more about today's scene, you need the no-nonsense advice of a Certified Management Consultant like Davidson. From his extensive files of actual case experiences he shares wise insights for aspiring entrepreneurs.

Retail Price: $10.95 • Special Price: $9.95

Trade • 6" x 9" • 260 pgs • ISBN: 1-56171-011-3

HUNT/KILL SELLING: *Sales Secrets Of The Professional Persuaders*
by Jack Matthews

This is a valuable tool for everyone involved in selling. 40 yrs. of sales secrets by America's top sales traner are revealed here.

If you want increased salesmanship from your sales team or from yourself, this is the ultimate book you must read!

Retail Price: $19.95 • Special Price: $14.95

Hard • 6" x 9" • 264 pgs • ISBN: 0-944007-78-3

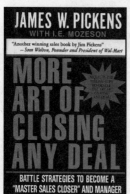

MORE ART OF CLOSING ANY DEAL • James Pickens

This book offers clever, gutsy and even slightly devious techniques that will bring you success at the closing table. You learn: the right and wrong times for managers to step in and help salesmen with customers; dozens of sure-fire techniques, deadly traps and imaginative ruses that sales closers and managers can coordinate; what all sales closers must know about managers–and vice versa.

Retail Price: $18.95 • Special Price: $17.95

Hard • 6" x 9" • 276 pgs • ISBN: 0-944007-58-9

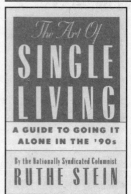

THE GUGGENHEIMS: *An American Epic* • by John Davis

The Guggenheims have left their mark on American cultural history through generations of philanthropy. The world famous Guggenheim museum is a testament to their taste and foresight. Now, John Davis (author of The Kennedys: Dynasty and Disaster, S.P.I.) chronicles the lives and times of the family that influenced the modem world more than any other through their vast philanthropic contributions and artistic insight.

Retail Price: $5.99 • Special Price: $4.99

Soft • 4" x 7" • 512 pgs • ISBN: 1-56171-351-1

THE HOFFA WARS
by Dan Moldea

The true story of the mafia's involvement in the disappearance of labor leader and teamster boss, Jimmy Hoffa. Author Dan Moldea has meticulously researched this unsolved crime and here reveals what really happend and how the Mob got away with this murder.

Retail Price: $5.99 • Special Price: $4.99

Soft • 4" x 7" • 498 pgs • ISBN: 1-56171-200-0

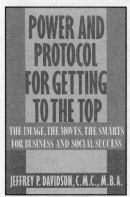

POWER AND PROTOCOL FOR GETTING TO THE TOP: *The Image, The Moves, The Smarts For Business And Social Success*
by Jeffrey Davidson

Ability & advanced degrees aren't enouugh to get you to the top–you have to talk, walk, dress & think like the power people who are in charge. You'll learn all the techniques to develop your own personal image of power.

Retail Price: $19.95 • Special Price: $14.95

Hard • 6" x 9" • 246 pgs • ISBN: 0-944007-68-6

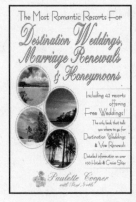

The Most Romantic Resorts For
Destination Weddings, Marriage Renewals & Honeymoons

Including 42 resorts offering Free Weddings!

The only book that tells you where to go for Destination Weddings & Vow Renewals

Detailed information on over 135 Hotels & Cruise Ships

Paulette Cooper with Paul North

THE MOST ROMANTIC RESORTS FOR DESTINATION WEDDINGS, MARRIAGE RENEWALS & HONEYMOONS • Paulette Cooper

The first book to tell you everything you need to know about destination weddings, marriage renewals, and honeymoon packages offered by more than 135 elegant hotels and cruise ships in the Caribbean, Mexico, Hawaii and U.S. The first book to tell you which resorts will marry you or renew your vows FOR FREE if you stay there. The first book that reveals what hundreds of people really thought about the resorts after staying there.

Retail Price: $5.99 • Special Price: $4.99

Paper • 8.5" x 11" • 304 pgs • Photos • ISBN: 1-56171-914-5

PLEASE NOTE: U.S. ORDERS–ADD $3.50 SHIPPING FOR 1st BOOK PLUS $1.00 PER EACH ADD'L BOOK. *(NON-U.S. ORDERS: $7.00 FOR 1st BOOK PLUS $2.00 PER ADD'L BOOK.)*

S.p.i. BOOKS

TITLE	QTY.	PRICE	TOTAL
(Please make checks payable to: S.P.I. Books) SUBTOTAL:			
For NY & MD shipments add sales tax:			
U.S. Shipping: $3.50 for 1st book plus $1.00 per add'l book.			
GRAND TOTAL: (Canadian res: only checks drawn on banks in the U.S. are accepted):			$

**Copy this page as your order form–then mail, fax or phone it in!
U.S. orders should arrive in 10 business days or less**

Indicate Method of Payment: M/C ☐(16 digits) VISA ☐(13 or 16 digits) Check/Money Order ☐

| Credit Card Number (min. charge $20.00) | | | | | | | | | | | | | | | | | Card Exp. Date: Mo. | | Yr. | |

Signature:
(Required, or we can't ship): 1 2 3 4 5 6 7 8 9 10 11 12 13 14 15 16

Name of Cardholder (print):

Credit Card Billing Address:

City/State/Zip:

Daytime Telephone (in case your order isn't clear):

Shipping Address for UPS: (same)☐

City/State/Zip for UPS: (same)☐

E-mail address:

**MAIL ORDERS TO: S.P.I. Books c/o, Dunst Fulfillment
106 Competitive Goals Dr., Eldersberg, MD 21784**

For Fast, Easy Service:
Order by **phone 24 hours:**
800-545-8146 or (410) 549-3946
or **Fax** us your order:
(410) 549-3946
or **E-mail** us at:
portia@dunst.com
or **SEND A CHECK** to:
*S.P.I. Books c/o, Dunst Fulfillment
106 Competitive Goals Dr.,
Eldersberg, MD 21784*
For Questions call our
Editorial Office: (212) 431-5011